I Am Positive

Katie Peters

GRL Consultants,
Diane Craig and Monica Marx,
Certified Literacy Specialists

Pull Ahead Readers People Smarts

Lerner Publications ◆ Minneapolis

Note from a GRL Consultant
This Pull Ahead leveled book has been carefully designed for beginning readers. A team of guided reading literacy experts has reviewed and leveled the book to ensure readers pull ahead and experience success.

Lerner Publications Company
An imprint of Lerner Publishing Group, Inc.
241 First Avenue North
Minneapolis, MN 55401 USA

For reading levels and more information, look up this title at www.lernerbooks.com.

Main body text set in Memphis Pro 24/39
Typeface provided by Linotype.

Photo Acknowledgments
The images in this book are used with the permission of: © ArtBoyMB/Getty Images, pp. 10–11, 16 (hockey stick); © BrandyTaylor/Getty Images, pp. 4–5, 16 (baseball bat); © FatCamera/Getty Images, pp. 6–7, 8–9, 12–13, 16 (soccer ball); © kali9/Getty Images, pp. 14–15; © skodonnell/Getty Images, p. 3.

Front cover: © FatCamera/Getty Images

Library of Congress Cataloging-in-Publication Data

Names: Peters, Katie, author.
Title: I am positive / Katie Peters.
Description: Minneapolis : Lerner Publications, [2022] | Series: Character builders (Pull ahead readers people smarts - nonfiction) | Includes index. | Audience: Ages 4–7 | Audience: Grades K–1 | Summary: "Show children that playing on a sports team is an opportunity to practice having a good attitude even when the team loses. Pairs with the fiction title A Beautiful Day"— Provided by publisher.
Identifiers: LCCN 2020015135 (print) | LCCN 2020015136 (ebook) | ISBN 9781728403519 (library binding) | ISBN 9781728423326 (paperback) | ISBN 9781728417820 (ebook)
Subjects: LCSH: Sportsmanship—Juvenile literature. | Team sports—Juvenile literature.
Classification: LCC GV706.3 .P46 2021 (print) | LCC GV706.3 (ebook) | DDC 796—dc23

LC record available at https://lccn.loc.gov/2020015135
LC ebook record available at https://lccn.loc.gov/2020015136

Manufactured in the United States of America
2-1009211-48889-2/1/2023

Table of Contents

I Am Positive

My baseball team lost.

My basketball team lost.

My soccer team lost.

My hockey team lost.

My swim team lost.

But I have fun with my team!

What is something good about your day today?

Did You See It?

baseball bat

hockey stick

soccer ball

Index